MIKE STERNAD

WHEN, GOD?

UNDERSTANDING GOD'S TIMING IN A FAST-PACED WORLD

WHEN, GOD?
UNDERSTANDING GOD'S TIMING IN A FAST-PACED WORLD

BY MIKE STERNAD

Mailing Address:
Calvary Chapel Mobile,
312 T Schillinger Rd. S, Mobile, Alabama 36608

Website: www.calvarychapelmobile.com
Email: mikesternad@gmail.com

Copyright © 2020 by Mike Sternad
First edition.
ISBN: 978-1-7343454-3-8

All rights reserved. No part of this publication may be reproduced, stored in a retrieval system, or transmitted in any form or by any means without the express written consent of Mike Sternad.

Unless otherwise indicated, Scripture quotations in this book are taken from the New King James Version of the Bible. Copyright © 1979, 1980, 1982 by Thomas Nelson, Inc., Publishers. Used by permission.

Published by Contented Life Publishing
Printed in the United States of America

Edited by Miriam Rogers
Cover Design by Ashley Garcia
Interior Design by Ulrika Towgood

TABLE OF CONTENTS

FOREWORD 5

PREFACE 6

INTRODUCTION 8

CHAPTER 1: WHEN ARE WE GOING? 13

CHAPTER 2: CAN YOU GO FASTER? 21

CHAPTER 3: HOW MANY NAPS? 29

CHAPTER 4: ARE YOU WORKING TODAY? 35

CHAPTER 5: WHY DO I HAVE TO WAIT? 41

CHAPTER 6: ARE WE THERE YET? 47

CONCLUSION 51

ABOUT THE AUTHOR 54

FOREWORD

One of the most difficult things for us as Christians is waiting. We hate it. Oh, we may appreciate the theoretical understanding that it is good to wait on the Lord. However, so often actually having to wait can be sheer misery. Most of us know the scripture from Isaiah that says something about waiting, and eagles, and young men ... that we grow stronger by waiting on the Lord. But in reality, none of us like to wait. Why is that?

In this book, Mike does an excellent job of dealing with the topic of waiting. As he breaks down the challenges we face in a season of waiting, you will find yourself discovering the beauty and purpose of waiting on God. And as you read through this book and answer the reflection questions, you will begin to experience the practical promise, given in Isaiah, attached to waiting on the Lord—you will grow stronger!

Paul Hammontree
Associate Pastor
Mountain Life Calvary Chapel
Edwards, CO

PREFACE

I wrote this short book to help you understand that God's timing is perfect. As human beings living in a hurry up generation, it is difficult to wait for anything! From the DMV to the drive-thru, we do not like when things take long. There is a reason why Walmart delivery and Amazon same-day delivery are so popular! There is little to no waiting involved. I mean, we deserve to order something and have it arrive at our homes the same day, right? We deserve to have smooth service and get our food in less than three minutes, right? Amazon is my best friend as long as they deliver my package the same day. If not, point me to the person I can yell at! The problem with always being in a hurry is that while we are in a rush, we end up getting ahead of the Lord in this life. Instead of the Lord going before us, we end up going before Him and usurping His authority.

So often, our timing does not line up with God's timing because God often goes too slow from our human perspective. He does go before us but often He doesn't run; He slow walks us through life. If we are attempting to rush God even as He tells us to slow down and take a breath, it can leave us down and in despair. We quit praying and we want to give up on what we were hoping for. If the Lord gives us a promise, we sometimes carry over our impatience to the spiritual realm and we want that promise to be fulfilled yesterday, instead of waiting on God's perfect timing today. How can we have patience to wait on God? How can we not get frustrated when our timing isn't lining up with His timing? How do we have settled hearts when we seem to be waiting forever for the Lord's plans to come to pass?

I hope that while reading this book you will learn to trust in God's timing and wait upon Him with peaceful expectancy. He knows all and He knows best. Things may take a bit longer than you want, but if God says, "Not now," we should say OK. May we trust the Lord in those moments when He calls us to wait on Him. Following the Lord can often be like that red light, green light game we played as kids. You want to cross the finish line quickly, but you have no control of what is called out! Sometimes it seems like the red and yellow light are being called out too much and you just want a perpetual and consistent green light because, after all, time is a commodity!

There are a multitude of benefits of waiting upon the Lord's timing. One main truth to grasp is that the Lord works on our hearts as we wait for His promises to come to pass. You can be sure that if God gives you a promise, it will happen. You just have to trust Him during the waiting time. In every situation the Lord knows when things need to occur. *WHEN, GOD?* should be an ongoing prayer, and when the Lord gives you the answer, rest in that answer, whatever it is, and know that the Lord always knows best.

INTRODUCTION

On the West Coast, everyone is in a rush every day, all the time! People are so rushed they don't even push you out of the way because they don't realize you exist. It seems as if the majority of people are just trying to make it through the day and get to all their appointments on time. Life is measured by time and there is never enough hours in the day. When making plans with people, they must be made weeks or months in advance, or it's not going to happen. That's just how life is. It is nonstop. The faster a person's day goes, the more they fit into the culture of Southern California. It's just how it's been for a long time. If you are walking slow, you will be trampled on by those who are sprinting through life. I did not realize how West Coast culture was like until my family and I moved to Mobile, Alabama.

Since we moved to the Deep South in the summer of 2017, what a crazy change of pace it has been! It is like going into slow motion in contrast to the hyper speed pace that we were used to. Honestly, it was so surreal we couldn't handle it at first. We often became frustrated because people would drive slowly, move slow, and not rush at all! Moving slow in life was antithetical to what we thought life was supposed to be like. Now after living here in the Deep South for a while, we have become acclimated. What an amazing blessing that we don't have to strive to survive anymore. We are not crazily running around like headless chickens trying to strive to survive and we are no longer tense and as intense. We can breathe easier and move slower—and that's such a good thing!

In Mobile, Alabama, people take their time. It seems as if they actually want to listen to what you have to say. When we first moved here, we would be invited to people's homes and eat dinner, and then converse for a long time! It was refreshing that it never seemed like anyone was in a rush. Sometimes I'd have to drop something off or pick something up at a person's home and I'd go with the intention of getting this task done quickly. More often than not I'd leave the person's presence an hour later because we got talking about life! This was new to me. People seemed to care about what is going on with you. Who would have thought!

Even at work I'd find myself getting caught up in a conversation with someone by the coffee maker, and an hour later I've drank my coffee and realize I'd been in conversation for a long while. The very thing that seemed like a big inconvenience to me when we first moved here became something I have learned to appreciate. People take their time and they feel no need to rush. Even if it seems like they should rush, they still take their time and are not stressed out. I've grown to love this way of life because it causes me to calm down, relax and not be so in a hurry all the time. It's been a while since I've been back to Los Angeles. I'd be curious to see how it would be for me to travel back there and be reminded of what the way of life is like. I think people may see me as a bit calmer. I'd probably realize how people lack patience because they just feel like they have to get stuff done quickly. They're always racing against time; time seems to be too short for everyone. The West Coast thought is that people don't like to wait because if they're waiting, they are not progressing in life.

Life can be fast-paced and stress-filled. We try to beat the clock and get it all done right now. Sometimes we have to wait, and it drives us mad. We want it all now, yet God tells us to slow down. His timing is perfect. When we attempt to force things and move things along faster than God wants, we are in danger of getting ahead of God. When God calls us to move forward and we stay still, we are in danger of being out of sync with His timing.

Being out of line with the Lord's timing can steer us off the road of God's will. If we are not constantly seeking the Lord for His timing, we could end up stranded and alone. The Bible often talks about how God goes before us. If we aren't sticking close behind Him, the separation between us and the Lord will widen. If we are always in a rush and trying to run ahead of the Lord, then we will leave Him behind and not know where to go or what to do!

Why do many believers struggle with God's timing? Why do so many Christians feel discouraged when they have to wait longer than they'd like for God's promises to come to pass? I believe that if we truly became in sync with God's timing, we'd have heart rest and peace of mind. In Ecclesiastes 3:1 it says, "To everything there is a season, a time for every purpose under heaven."

From season to season the Lord works in our lives as we are willing to let Him lead. As God leads, we hear Him and heed His perfect timing. The *when* question is answered as we are in close communication with the Lord. God's timing is not a guessing game on our part, it's an intentional effort on our part to make sure we are in step with the timing of our Creator.

Our natural response for waiting on God is impatience and even anger. And yet, the Word of God speaks of the benefits of waiting upon the Lord. Just because the Lord has you waiting for a promise to be fulfilled doesn't mean He doesn't care or has put you off. If God has given a promise, you can be sure it will be fulfilled in His timing. So the question is, "When, God?" When will You fulfill that promise? What do I do while I'm waiting for that promise to be fulfilled? How do I know when You want me to wait, slow down, or move forward? When do I know if I've skirted ahead of You, Lord? When do I know when I'm lagging behind? These questions and more are answered in this book from a biblical truth-filled standpoint.

Throughout *When, God?* you will discover the various questions pertaining to God's timing. At the end of each chapter you will also find questions designed to help you better understand God's timing and how you can be faithful to adhere to it. My hope is that as you apply these lessons, you may find yourself being in sync with the timeline your Creator has set for you and therefore, find rest for your soul.

"But those who wait on the LORD shall renew their strength; they shall mount up with wings like eagles, they shall run and not be weary, they shall walk and not faint."
—Isaiah 40:31

CHAPTER 1

WHEN ARE WE GOING?

A man's heart plans his way, but the LORD directs his steps.

PROVERBS 16:9

WHEN MY DAUGHTERS WERE really little, they didn't care about when things happened because they had no concept or concern about time. They just wanted to play. Now that they are older, they are at that stage where they have 1,001 questions about everything, including time. This is why when we are planning a vacation, we don't tell them where we are going weeks in advance. My wife makes sure I say nothing about where we are going because then my daughters would ask their mom, "When are we going?" every day until the time we actually go! Kids want to know when things are going to happen, especially if the event happens to be an exciting adventure.

Most of us adults want to know when as well. When will God move me to a better job? When will the Lord get me to the end of this horrible trial? When will the pain go away? When will I hear from God? When will the Lord speak to me and bring me from where I am now to where I want to be? We constantly want to know when God will move us from where we are because oftentimes where we are is not bringing contentment to our hearts. We are often unsettled where we are presently, and so we wonder when things will change or get better.

As believers, we are often so focused on the future that we lose sight of what God's doing right now. We feel like there's no forward motion in our lives so we wonder when the Lord will alter our circumstances for the better. In my experience, God's timing is much slower than my timing. Much. Slower. I want to get a move on before the Lord even tells me to get up and walk forward. I can plan my future all day long but without the Lord's leading, I'd be planning in vain!

God wants to be a part of our plans and He wants to be involved in our planning process. If we make plans apart from our Father's leading, we will end up at an earthly location rather than a divine destination. It will not end well. God's plans for our future are perfect and He's always presently preparing us to walk in His promises.

When I began serving the Lord at a church I was attending, I wanted everything to move quickly and I ended up going ahead of the Lord. I wanted to hurry up and do my time teaching the youth so I could be a pastor to adults. As the years went by and I kept teaching the youth, I realized that I wasn't giving these kids my whole heart because I was so future focused, I wasn't really presently there. The youth group was getting ripped off because I was so focused on what *could* be rather than on what was. Once I planted both my feet into the season of opportunity at hand, then I saw God move in mighty ways. When Paul talks about "redeeming the time" in Ephesians 5:16, he is saying that whatever season you're in right now is a time where God wants to use you the most! You will be eternally productive where God has you presently.

Before I began walking with the Lord, I was a manager at all five jobs I have previously had. In those jobs it was all about having a sense of urgency and working hard, and the result was moving up quickly. This happened for me at every job because I was acting on goal setting and getting things done! So I brought this mentality into the church because I had no clue how it worked. I was goal setting for God and getting things done for God's kingdom the way I knew how. It was how I knew life worked in the world, but not necessarily in the church. So in my mind, things took so long to happen and went much slower than I was used to.

I began serving the Lord by sweeping the pathway that led to the front door of the church. I took pride in this because I knew it was for the Lord and it would bless people. At first I was so excited to get to church and sweep with all my heart. I wanted to make sure that I swept every single leaf out of the way and did the best I could because it was all for the Lord! I swept for a few months and then I began helping to set up the sound before church and break down the equipment after church. With each new task I was asked to help with, I would be so happy. The more faithful I was, the more God gave me to do. I was given a bunch of little tasks, and soon I was super busy at church, taking on a lot of responsibility.

Looking back, I remember there were times where I was serving with discontentment because I kept asking the question, "When, God?" I'd be setting up or breaking down, and it was great, but I often wanted to do more. I wanted to do something different. I wanted God to hurry up and add some more stuff to be faithful with because this wasn't enough. I thought, *when in the world is the Lord going to give me more responsibility? I can handle it! Bring it on!* Then the Lord allowed me certain opportunities that I wasn't ready for, just to show me that I needed to be content right where I was at, with what He had given me to do. I can say I am so glad God taught me to wait on the *when* and slow down.

When we are in a rush, that's when we become anxious and discouraged. When we are in a hurry all the time, in a sense we leave God behind and begin to construct our own timetable. My whole Christian life I've been learning to slow down and allow God to lead, rather than jump ahead of Him and act like I know where I'm going without Him.

My oldest daughter, Hannah, is very task-oriented. Every morning she wants to know what is going to happen that day and when it's going to happen. Hannah is very much like me in that she is goal-oriented, and if given a challenge she will step up to it and get it done within the required amount of time. Hannah needs to know the details. So if she has no clue when things are going to happen, frustration will creep into her little mind and she will become anxious and frustrated. Our daughters measure everything by naps. If we say we're going on vacation, they would ask, "How many naps is that?" It is difficult for Hannah when she doesn't know how many naps until something will occur in the future. As we grow older, oftentimes we can be just as impatient as our kids when it comes to the Lord's timetable.

When we view God's timing as an opportunity for our spiritual life to grow and accept the truth that waiting on God is part of the Christian life, we have the right perspective. God doesn't give us promises and then say wait just to see us squirm. He works on our hearts in the waiting and He equips us for what's ahead. We don't like this though! We want to jump the gun, get ahead of the Lord and continue to ask, "When are we going?!"

God says wait, and we ask why? We must learn to wait on God for each promise that He gives us.

Oftentimes people get impatient and act unchristian when they have to wait too long. Have you ever been in a line and the person in front of you seems like they're going to lose it if they have to wait any longer? Or maybe you've been that person who got upset because what should have been a five-minute wait has turned into a fifty-minute wait. Have you been to the DMV? The goal for us as believers is to truly trust that the Lord's timing is the best timing. He may have given a promise to you that is not even close to coming to pass. Be okay with the slow work of God and know that the Lord has some heart preparing to do in you before that promise comes to fruition! The answer to the question, "When are we going?" is *when the Lord gives the green light.*

WHEN ARE WE GOING?
QUESTIONS FOR REFLECTION

1. We are not to be so future focused that we lose sight of where God has us presently. Read the passage in Matthew 6:25-34. According to verse 34, why are we to focus on today rather than tomorrow?

_____

_____

_____

_____

2. Oftentimes we are called to wait upon the Lord after He has given us a promise. What does the psalmist tell us to do as we wait upon the Lord in Psalm 62:5? And how does the psalmist describe the Lord in verses 6 and 7?

_____

_____

_____

_____

CHAPTER 2

CAN YOU GO FASTER?

Rest in the LORD, and wait patiently for Him; do not fret because of him who prospers in his way, because of the man who brings wicked schemes to pass.

PSALM 37:7

MY GIRLS LOVE TO VISIT me at my office and when they do, they seem to like rearranging everything on my desk. They are curious about the various office supplies I use, and they touch everything. To this day I'm still missing a few items from my workspace that have magically disappeared. After moving everything around in my office, they proceed to get on my office chair and ask me to spin them. I'd spin them with all my might and they'd still say the same thing over and over again: "Can you go faster?! Faster, Daddy!" I'd keep spinning that office chair as fast as I could but there is a certain point where if that chair were spun any faster, it may fly off the base! So I usually have to say, "Girls, the chair does not go any faster than that!"

As believers it's difficult when things don't move as fast as we'd like! After all, we are Americans and we should not have to wait more than five minutes for anything, right?! It is very difficult when goals, life circumstances, and to-do lists take much longer than we want. When I was younger, I worked at Jamba Juice on Main street in Venice, California, and when serving up orders we had to have a sense of urgency. When someone ordered a smoothie, we would grab the blender, scoop in the fruit, ice, sorbet and ice cream, and pour in the juice as fast as we could! Then we had to throw the blender on high speed and mix the ingredients a bit, take it off the engine, bang the side, blend it more, pour it in the cup, put the lid on, wet the receipt and stick it to the side of the cup and hand it to the customer. I'm tired just explaining it! But we had to move fast, especially when we had a rush. A sense of urgency was part of the job.

When it comes to the Christian life, we often want God to move as fast as He can to fulfill His will in us! We're like children telling God to move faster than His will actually requires. Now we don't necessarily tell God to move faster or complain when His timetable differs from ours, but we do wonder why things are taking so long. We have deadlines in our minds but our goals usually do not line up with God's perfect timing.

There are seasons where God moves quickly and we're trying to keep up. We take steps of faith and things fall into place fast! Usually, though, God takes much longer than we want Him to take. We desire God's will to be like fast food, same-day delivery or microwavable meals. The reality is that God's timeline is different than Amazon Prime. If we received everything from God quickly, then we would *not* be prepared for those future promises.

It takes time for the Lord to prepare us for future endeavors. At a conference years ago, a pastor said something very simple and profound that stuck with me. He said, "We need to trust in the slow work of God." It was both difficult and eye-opening for me to hear because it is the opposite of my fast-paced mindset. It's not that God moves too slow, it's that I move too fast and want God to keep up! We often jump ahead of God when the Bible says over and over that God goes before us. The Lord never says, "I'll follow you"—instead He always says, "Follow Me." God leads our lives and we are called to obey, submit and yield to Him because He is the Lord and we are not. God moves at a pace that is perfect and it's our job to follow close behind Him. As He leads, He knows where He is going and He knows what He is doing. Sometimes we act as if this isn't the case and attempt to take our lives in our own hands, but often that does not end well. If we move too fast we'll be in danger of not walking by faith but instead forging ahead and crashing because of hastiness.

Running our race of faith doesn't mean we need to always sprint. There are moments where we must slow down, take a breath and assess where we are at in the context of God's will. The goal of the Christian life is to stay in the middle of the mission the Lord has for us. It reminds me of the apostle Paul as he was prevented from going north and south, and instead the Lord directed him west to Philippi. The Lord rerouted him because there was work to do in that city! Paul got what is referred to as the Macedonian call! God used Paul greatly as he planted a church in Philippi and marvelous work happened there. Paul had in mind to travel to certain locations but God had other plans. When we let God lead us according to His timing and direction, we will be exactly where God wants us to be at exactly the right time.

My two daughters are opposite in a lot of ways, especially when it comes to moving quickly. My older daughter, Hannah, will color a page in a coloring book just to get it done. Yes, it will be sloppy and messy but she will get done before her younger sister and announce, "Look, Daddy, I finished it!" To her it's a competition of who can get done first. My younger daughter, Lily, on the other hand, will color so slow, it will take a couple of hours for her to finish half a page!

When she's done though, all the colors will be within the lines; nothing is messy or sloppy about her coloring. Hannah eats fast like me. She will devour a few pieces of pizza in a short amount of time. It's actually impressive! Lily eats so slow that I often have to take deep breaths and pray to stay patient. My wife and I have never seen anyone eat so slow ever. Yes, Lily is definitely healthier because she actually chews her food, but I will often get impatient waiting for Lily to finish, especially at restaurants. My wife gives me this look: *Calm down, just wait, it's going to be OK*. My wife's looks are filled with information I could easily read. It always ends up being OK because Lily will eventually finish … or sometimes we would run out of time and get the rest of her food to go.

Often I find myself having to seek God for patience because of the slow work I feel He is doing. Living in the Deep South for the last few years really has slowed me down. I'm not running until I burn out like I did in Los Angeles; I take my time so much more. I love the way of life here because time is less hectic than in Southern California. I'm learning to slow down and enjoy where I'm at and what God is doing right now in the present. I've stopped being a clock watcher and instead, just let God run the time. When I do eventually go back and visit the West Coast, I think I may be shocked at how fast-paced it is. Being in the South has caused me to not be in such a rush and to slow down and enjoy life right now.

I believe God wants to do the same thing in our lives. Slow down, allow Him to work, and adhere to His timing. Let Him prepare you now for what He has for you in the future. Instead of asking: "God, can You go faster?" I think a better statement is: "God, I will stay right where You have me until You say go." May we let the Lord set the pace for our everyday lives and trust in the slow work of God. What we want faster is probably not as important as we think. What God wants for us now is what truly matters; the quicker we are OK with building God's kingdom where He has planted us, the quicker our hearts will be at peace and our lives content.

CAN YOU GO FASTER?
QUESTIONS FOR REFLECTION

1. So often we can attempt to speed up God's will, and it never works! Why should we remain patient and trust the slow work of God? Read James 5:7-8 in your Bible and answer this question.

_____

_____

_____

_____

2. We can be hasty from time to time. We attempt to rush God instead of waiting upon the Lord. What does the Bible say about being diligent as opposed to being hasty? Read Proverbs 21:5 in your Bible to answer this question. Give an example from your own experience.

_____

_____

_____

_____

CHAPTER 3

HOW MANY NAPS?

The LORD is good to those who wait for Him, to the soul who seeks Him. It is good that one should hope and wait quietly for the salvation of the LORD.

LAMENTATIONS 3:25-26

IT WAS LIKE A MIRACLE when our girls used to take naps in their younger years. My wife and I would have a good two hours to take a nap ourselves and rest. Those moments were so sweet for our health, marriage and sanity. We desperately needed them! It was amazing that we could cuddle on the couch and snooze for a while. Then our daughters stopped napping and we had to say *so long* to that two-hour window of rest time. Nowadays they are so unpredictable; they may take a nap or they may not depending on what they do that day.

My two daughters, who are six and seven years old as I'm writing this, measure everything in naps. If we are going on vacation, they don't want to know how many days until we leave; they want to know how many naps until we leave. And since they don't take naps anymore, a nap means one sleep at nighttime. So if we are going on vacation in three days, we tell them we are going in three naps. They understand that and it makes sense to them.

Just like my girls measure everything by naps, we measure life by how long everything takes. *How long will it take until God's promise in my life comes to pass? How long until my life goals come to fruition?*

Abraham and Sarah had to wait twenty-five years from the time they were given the promise of having a child to Isaac being born. They failed during that time because they were hasty rather than patient.

Moses was in the desert for forty years herding sheep when God spoke to him, calling him to lead millions of people out of slavery. He was eighty years old!

Jeremiah preached for decades with not one convert, yet the Word burned in his bones so he kept on preaching! The point is we are often given clear-cut promises but there is almost always a time of preparation before the promise comes to pass!

Society marks success by how quickly we can get things done and accomplish our goals. *We have to move forward. We must not stop. Keep striving. Never quit. We can rest when we're dead!* Sure, these sayings sound like pure motivation and good intentions, but this is not the way God designed us to be. Yes, we work for the Lord and stay in the middle of our God-given mission, but we also need to rest and wait on God. Much of the time, it is difficult to wait and we foolishly begin wrestling with the Lord. We question God because everything seems to be going way too slow! *How many naps until God brings me a wife? How many naps until I get that new job? How many naps until I get out of this horrible trial? How many naps until God provides for me?* See, we ask these questions not because we actually want the answer but because we want to find a way to speed things up.

While we are waiting on one promise, there is work for us to do. Paul makes it clear in Ephesians 5:16 that we are to redeem the time for the days are evil. So even if we are waiting for a God-given promise, we are to do what God wants us to do in the now. If we remain idle, we become too comfortable which leads to becoming complacent, which then leads to compromise. That is a dark but unfortunate common progression among Christians.

Instead of focusing on how long it might take the Lord to fulfill a promise to us, let's focus on where He has us at this very moment. Let's ask God what He wants us to do as we wait on that promise.

In the context of naps, it could take thousands of naps or countless nights before our hearts are prepared for God's future promises for us. May we patiently allow Him to prepare our hearts when it seems like things are moving at a snail's pace.

There may be moments where it feels like life is at a standstill. You must remember that heart work, wisdom and godly attributes are being built up in you during the waiting time. The promises of God will come to pass. But until then, take advantage of the slow season you're in right now. God is at work and He will continue to work even when you don't always see every detail. The Lord directs and leads you even if you don't know all the details or *when God* will reveal them to you. You just need to hear Him, let Him lead and follow accordingly. Be patient in the waiting. Allow God to fully prepare you now for His future promises!

HOW MANY NAPS?
QUESTIONS FOR REFLECTION

1. We often desire to know how long everything will take because we do not want anything to take longer than a few minutes. How do we get to a place where we fully trust God's timing and restrain the curiosity that causes us to be impatient? Read Psalm 37:3-4 in your Bible to answer this question.

_____

_____

_____

_____

2. God does not measure time in heaven like we measure time on earth. Is God stressed out because certain plans take too long? Read 2 Peter 3:8 in your Bible to answer this question.

_____

_____

_____

_____

CHAPTER 4

ARE YOU WORKING TODAY?

Trust in the LORD with all your heart, and lean not on your own understanding; in all your ways acknowledge Him, and He shall direct your paths.

PROVERBS 3:5-6

MY DAUGHTERS HATE THAT I have to leave to go to work. Almost every day they ask me if I'm going to work and five out of seven days I have to say, "Yes, Daddy has to work today." I proceed to assure them that the weekend is only a few naps away and then we can get a lot of family time! I explain to my girls that I have to work forty hours a week so we can eat food, have shelter, buy clothes and have fun. They understand at the time ... until the next day when we go through the whole routine again. They don't see me for about nine hours a day on weekdays, but they know where I am and what I'm doing. Work is how we live, eat and go on vacations together.

When it seems like God is taking a while to answer prayer or fulfill a promise, we sometimes wonder if He's still working. It may *feel* like God is absent or far off helping someone else. Like Kevin in the movie *Home Alone*, we feel we've been forgotten because of mistaken identity. There are moments when I begin to think these discouraging thoughts and I seek God through prayer and through His Word. I get reminded that yes, God is there, He hasn't forgotten about me and He is not far off! When we ask God, "Are You working today?" the answer is always a gigantic YES! The Lord is always working, whether we acknowledge it or not.

Trusting the Lord with all our hearts is not easy. But it's a necessity. Walking by faith can be the hardest action to take but it's the most blessed way to live. When we trust God we are saying, "Lord, I don't know the details but I know You're directing me!" It's easy to trust God when times are smooth and life seems carefree. Yet it's more difficult to fully trust God during those times where things seem undone, when we have big decisions to make, and when our future is on the line. It can be daunting just thinking about all the future events that we will have to face. We can become anxious in the waiting and in the way God is working.

When my family and I moved across the country from the West Coast to the Deep South, we *had* to trust the Lord with our whole hearts. We had no choice because this was a huge life change! If my wife and I had doubted God and tried to get a five-point plan from Him first, we would *not* have moved! God simply confirmed we were supposed to go and start a new work, and we went! With every step of faith God gave us another detail and we continued to take those steps fully trusting God. Has it been easy? Absolutely not! Is it a blessing? Totally! When we trust God with all of who we are, we will be blessed, amazed and awestruck that God would see fit to use you and me to accomplish His amazing purposes.

Leaning upon our own understanding will lead to discouragement; leaning upon God's understanding brings reassurance that He's at work! Periodically I'll tell my congregation that I do not know what I'm doing in leading the church. Now, you don't normally hear this statement from the pulpit because people may question your leadership and leave the church. Some probably have. But I say it to demonstrate that I am not the one running the church and making all the decisions—the Lord is! I don't have all the answers and that is precisely why I lean upon God's sovereignty and perfect plan. His ways are perfect!

I think it's dangerous to lean upon our own understanding because then we become self-sufficient instead of God-reliant. The pressure is off of us when we trust that God is in complete control of every aspect of our daily lives. Being omniscient or all-knowing, the Lord directs our hearts and faithfully leads us. He is literally a know-it-all! When God is the authority in our lives, we live in such a way that surrender is not an afterthought—it is a priority. Lean upon God's wisdom because the wisdom of man is *not* wisdom at all. God is at work and He works according to His timetable, which is flawless.

We must acknowledge that God is constantly on the move orchestrating our lives and getting His will done. My kids get in major trouble when they forget that they have parents. Don't get me wrong, they don't literally forget we exist but sometimes they act like they are the captain and leader of their own lives. So they temporarily cease to acknowledge that we are in charge. The result is not listening to us and attempting to lead themselves. They begin to believe they know it all; they are leaders, not the followers—and they get in trouble. We have to remind them that we are the parents and they are the children, not the other way around. The same is true with our relationship with the Lord. At times we live like He is not in control of our future. We forget to acknowledge God and we stray from the path of His will. We can get so wrapped up in our plans that we stop acknowledging that God's way is always the best way. We must acknowledge that God's plans, purposes and timing are completely impeccable.

Our life will be headed the right way when we surrender and allow God to lead our path! I think about my two young daughters and wonder what their path in life will be. Where will they go to college and what careers will they have? Who will they marry? As their dad sometimes it freaks me out thinking about these things. It's seriously scary because they are so young right now. Ultimately, my prayer is that my girls would cling to the Lord and follow His plan for them. I don't want to see my daughters trekking through life without God's leading and then having to take the long way around backtracking. They will have thousands of choices as to which road they could take in life. This is precisely a picture of our walk with God as well. There are so many choices we can make, there are so many ways we could go. Yet, there's only one way we should go and only one path we should want to be on—God's path! He knows the road we need to be on and the speed in which we should travel down that road. From our perspective, the one thing we must do daily is surrender. When we live a life poured out for the Lord, we can know that He is working. He does not stop working and He never will.

ARE YOU WORKING TODAY?
QUESTIONS FOR REFLECTION

1. It should reassure and comfort us to know that there is never a moment where God is not working. Sometimes God waits to work in certain areas, and we mistakenly think He doesn't care. What mindset should we have when it comes to knowing that God is working? Read Galatians 6:9.

_____

_____

_____

_____

2. We must walk by faith in the promises of God no matter how long we have to wait for the fulfillment. Read Psalm 27:14. What are the ways we can trust God's timing with the right heart?

_____

_____

_____

_____

CHAPTER 5

WHY DO I HAVE TO WAIT?

But those who wait on the LORD shall renew their strength; they shall mount up with wings like eagles, they shall run and not be weary, they shall walk and not faint.

ISAIAH 40:31

THE CONCEPT OF WAITING IS confusing for children. They don't understand that they can't have everything they want right this second. My daughters often want dessert before dinner, fun before school, and a show before reading their books. My wife and I will explain to them that some of the most amazing blessings are those we must wait for! I'm confident they will believe this one day. I remember when I was a kid, I desperately wanted a Mongoose BMX bike. I was saving my allowance from doing extra chores at home and I could not wait to buy that thing! Finally, the day came when I had enough money to buy this all-white BMX bike that had all the coolest accessories! It took a long time to save up the $200 for the bike, but when I finally bought it and brought it home and rode it through my apartment complex, it was all worth it!

Waiting on God is worth it. At this moment we may be waiting for some promises to come to pass and it may feel like we will be waiting forever. It can be frustrating but know that during the interim period God is seriously working! He is active in those moments even when it seems like He is absent. God is not idle or indifferent. Let me put it this way. Would you want a steak that is cooked in the microwave for five minutes and then slapped on your plate, or would you want a steak that's marinated, gently put on the grill and slowly seared to perfection? Oftentimes it takes time for God's perfect will to come to fruition. Our job as believers is to wait on His promises and yet still be active for the kingdom as we're waiting.

Strength often stems from and is built up during those God-given waiting periods. As we wait on God, we are practicing a fruit of the Spirit that is at the end of the Galatians 5:22-23 list: self-control. Just because it's listed at the end doesn't mean it's less important. We Americans tend to be huge consumers; instead of prayerfully pondering, we just tap our phones a couple times out of haste and buy it all! *Add to cart* times 10! Some may say self-control is for people who don't have any money or for people who have major addictions (so I'm all good). This is far from the truth! Generally speaking, instead of being rash and impulsive we must learn to be prayerful and methodical, or else we'll jump the gun and run ahead of the Lord. Our strength increases when we have to wait for a sure future promise. God prepares us in the midst of waiting so that when those promises come to pass, we will have strength to handle them!

As we wait on God, our hearts, our minds, and lives will be prepared. My daughters love going on family vacations. We often go to Orange Beach which is an hour drive from our house. They love the whole experience—packing their little backpacks with clothes and toys, making sure they have what they need, getting to the hotel, being amazed at the standard room we paid for, eating pizzas, swimming in the pool, and just being together. Even though these may only be two-night trips, we still need to prepare for them. I have to request time off from work, my wife has to not schedule any playdates or meet-ups with her friends, and we have to make sure our girls don't have dance, ballet, t-ball or swimming lessons on the days we'll be gone. In other words, we have to do some preparation before we drive off and enjoy our time together! Same thing with God's promises. During those waiting periods, we must allow

God to prepare our hearts so when the time is right, we'll be ready to enjoy those promises! God renews our strength as we wait upon Him.

Let's face it, at times we feel tired, weary and burned out, like my wife and I do after we've been on vacation with our incredible and active daughters. These are moments when we need to rest in order for rejuvenation to happen. So don't despise those moments of waiting upon God, they are purposeful in us gaining God's supernatural strength!

After God rejuvenates you in the waiting you'll be able to run unhindered. Our daughters love to play chase. That's really all they want to do when I'm watching them at home. They will run and run and run some more! I will run and run and then take a break, catch my breath and drink some water as I'm wheezing. Running with my daughters makes me realize I am not super young and full of energy anymore. I need breaks to rest so I can play chase with my girls for a longer period of time! If I didn't rest to catch my breath and gain my stamina back, I'd probably pass out and my girls would have to hit the emergency button on my iPhone to get help. God didn't rest on the seventh day for nothing. He did it to give us an example of what we should do on a regular basis. In order to have strength to fulfill God's will, we must remember to rest in Him before we run our race of faith.

As we gain strength in the waiting, our weariness is wiped out! Weariness is a serious problem in our culture today. People run until they are out of steam; they strive to the point of exhaustion, completely burned out! My daughters do the same exact thing! They like to play all day every day and they get to the point where their eyes cannot stay open and they practically pass out! On a typical day, the girls will do homeschooling in the morning, then Mama will take them to the community pool to swim in the southern sun for hours, next they'll run errands, or they'll have a playdate with friends from church and probably go get Chick-fil-A. And on the drive home from all that, they are done. Their eyes can't help but to close, heads tilted, mouths open, passed out from weariness. "The dishes are done, man!" (Adventures in Babysitting). Now this may be a common pattern for kids as they are growing and developing, but this is not a good routine for a grown Jesus believer!

God often calls us to rest in the time of waiting as He equips us for the next excursion He has planned for us. Many times we disregard the benefit of rest and instead, continue to run our race when in reality, God wants us to sit down, get some fluids, take a breath and take care of ourselves. We were not made to run until we're burned out. We were made to run when God says go, and rest awhile when God says wait. Many times it takes self-control to slow down and just be in the present, being fully aware of our surroundings and letting our minds and bodies rest! If we keep going non-stop, we'll remain in the state of burnout and end up getting discouraged and defeated all the time! Rest in the waiting. Take a breath while relaxing. Enjoy those moments of stillness and realize God's blessings. Do not forget the importance of kicking back and reflecting on how good God is while you are waiting on His promises.

WHY DO I HAVE TO WAIT?
QUESTIONS FOR REFLECTION

1. Waiting upon God is one of the most difficult actions to take because we think faster is better. But sometimes God wants us to wait so He can equip us and teach us His attributes. What has God taught you during those long moments of waiting? Refer to Psalm 25:4-5 to answer this question.

_____

_____

_____

_____

2. Sometimes as we are waiting upon God, it seems that He is silent. But that is far from the truth. How do we know the Lord hears us during those moments when we are waiting upon His promises? What does Micah 7:7 tell us?

_____

_____

_____

_____

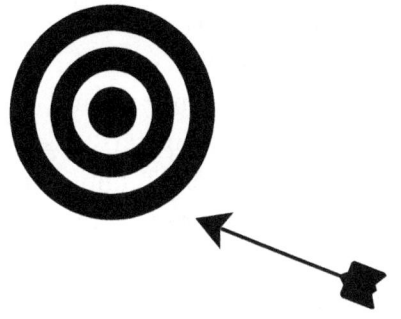

CHAPTER 6

ARE WE THERE YET?

But, beloved, do not forget this one thing, that with the Lord one day is as a thousand years, and a thousand years as one day. The Lord is not slack concerning His promise, as some count slackness, but is longsuffering toward us, not willing that any should perish but that all should come to repentance.

2 PETER 3:8-9

OUR YOUNG DAUGHTERS HAVE no concept of time. One time we had an opportunity to make the nine-hour drive from Mobile to Disney World in Orlando. Thirty minutes in, our daughters asked, "Are we there yet?" It was funny at first until they continued to ask this same question every ten minutes. We finally let them know it is a long drive and asking that question would not speed things up. But after the trek from Lower Alabama to South Florida, we pulled up to Disney World and the girls were so ecstatic! It was our first time and we could see on their faces that their dreams had come true! It was a blessing as parents to witness such joy on their faces and happiness in their hearts. The drive was arduous and the girls so restless but once we arrived at our destination, their exhaustion turned into excitement and restlessness turned into real joy!

When it comes to God's timing, we can become restless and impatient. God has given us the destination; we know our future will be in heaven but it's the journey that seems daunting at times. We have to go through some boring driving before we get to our God-given destination. God hears our questioning as we often ask, "Are we there yet?" As avid followers of Jesus we seem to think if we nag God enough, He will speed things up. Not so! We must plant our feet where God has us presently and trust that He will get us to the destination in His timing. And when we get to our God-given destination and the Lord fulfills His promises, our elation will be evident, and we'll be so incredibly excited! But shouldn't the journey be exciting as well?

The journey will be exciting when your heart is fully trusting God. Our divine path doesn't have to be a monotonous, boring and depressing time. The adventure of being in God's will is exciting if we see it as a venture of faith, rather than a holding cell. If we are only focused on the end goal, then the present path we are on will lack joy and expectancy.

We have to constantly teach our daughters to embrace their present blessings rather than always looking for something more. They get so focused on what they're going to do tomorrow that they forget they are so being blessed in the present. We'll be at a hotel pool in Orange Beach swimming. They are laughing and having a blast. Then one of them will ask, "What are we doing after this?" Or, "How many more days do we have here?" My wife and I have to remind them to not dwell on what we'll do later or the next day, but rather enjoy what we are doing at this very moment!

We can do the same thing! The life of a believer is all about learning to be expectant for the future but also being excited for the present. None of us have yet arrived at our final destination. I believe that the Lord desires that we long for the destination but He also wants us to enjoy the journey! If we let impatience go unchecked, we will be miserable in the now. In other words, if we are not fully engaged in where God has us this moment, then we'll be left unhappy and unfulfilled. There are definitely future promises we're waiting for at this time but that doesn't mean we should put our lives on hold and stop living. The future is bright for the believer but so is the present as long as we stay in the middle of God's mission for us! Your future is bright but don't forget to find joy in the journey. You may not be there yet, but take heart, child of God, you will get there. Trust God's timing. It will be worth it.

ARE WE THERE YET?
QUESTIONS FOR REFLECTION

1. As believers, God's will for us seems to take a long time to unfold. Yet still our hearts should be expectant for what God is going to do. What does the Bible say about expecting God to move? Read 1 Corinthians 2:9-10 in your Bible to answer this question.

_____

_____

_____

_____

2. We must embrace the present blessings or we will always be way too future focused to be happy in the current circumstances. What are some reasons we should bless God and rest in our present blessings?

Read Psalm 103:2 and Psalm 119:2 in your Bible to find this answer.

_____

_____

_____

_____

CONCLUSION

To everything there is a season, a time for every purpose under heaven. —**Ecclesiastes 3:1**

My wife and I were married on June 24th, 2006. A couple years had gone by as we were trying to finish college and work fairly good jobs. Brianne wanted children so badly she had cried about it countless times. As we were seeking the Lord about His timing for starting a family, I just knew we had to wait. A few more years went by and she still desperately wanted kids. I knew it wasn't God's timing yet and so we often got in heated discussions about starting a family. This pattern continued for six years after we were married. Finally, God gave the green light and we had two children. Now that we have our two daughters, my wife reflects back to that time when she desperately wanted babies. As she thought about it she told me one day, "I was not ready to have kids when we had those heated discussions. It was just a desire of my heart for a future moment that I wanted sooner than the Lord's timing. I didn't want to wait." She went on to say, "I am so glad you said no all those times!" It was hard to see my wife weep and hear her long for children. But I knew God wanted us to wait. He wanted to work on our hearts and prepare and equip us before we had children. God's timing is absolutely perfect.

Waiting on God was difficult but it was the right thing to do. After we were married, we had six full years to grow closer to God and to one another. We became best friends during that time. When we got married, almost every married couple told us not to have kids right away and enjoy one another as long as we could. Of course we were led by God to wait but what these married couples said rang true as well! If we were going to be good and godly parents, we needed to be connected and cohesive as a couple and strong in the Lord—and that takes time!

In those six years we grew closer to the Lord and closer to one another. Brianne and I sought God alone and as a couple. We went on many vacations up and down the West Coast and we spent a lot of time together! Looking back, we both realize that God was preparing us and setting us up for what He had planned for us in the future! We are so blessed that we waited on God for six years to have children. We grew in our faith and therefore, grew closer to one another. So by the time we had our two daughters we were ready because God prepared us in our one-on-one relationship with Him and in our relationship with one another. We were on the same page; we saw eye to eye and we were of the same mind and aligned with God!

When you're in the middle of waiting, it can be so difficult. You may get anxious and even angry that you have to wait. You may be kicking and screaming like a little child because you want what you want, and you want it now! But the best action to take when

God calls you to wait is inaction. What I mean is when God lays it on your heart clearly to wait, even though you don't want to, you must practice self-control and just wait for the green light from the Lord! The worst thing to do is run the red light anyway! Rushing God could cause a major wreck in your life. God knows the timing of everything. Trust Him in the waiting. Trust in the slow work of God for He is preparing you for when the light turns green. Take a breath, relax your shoulders, and learn to be content in the place where you are at presently. God's the leader, you are the follower. Embrace the truth that God's timing is perfect and He knows what's best for you.

ABOUT THE AUTHOR

Mike Sternad is the senior pastor of Calvary Chapel Mobile in Mobile, Alabama, a church he planted in September 2017. At the heart of this ministry is a strong focus on teaching the Word of God and sharing it with as many people as possible. Mike believes that he himself is proof of the power of God's Word to transform a lost and broken individual into a blessed man, husband and father. He and his wife, Brianne, have two daughters, Hannah and Lily.

To see more of what Mike has written,
visit www.mikesternad.com